Weight Watchers New Complete Cookbook 2021

200+ Quick and Easy WW SmartPoints Recipes to Transform Your Body and Lose Weight

Keri Eichorn

Table of Contents

Introduction

Weight Watchers International Inc. is the most promising, effective, successful, and largest diet program specifically designed for weight loss. The company was initially formed by a woman named and has been growing globally for the past six decades. Smart Point is a numeric system that is based on counting in the Weight Watchers Program. It utilizes the principles of modern nutritional science and makes weight loss easier. It inclines you to have healthier and nutritious foods to ensure a sound, healthy, energetic lifestyle and of course weight loss. In this numeric system, every food is credited with a particular value which is based on four main things that include sugar, calories, protein, and saturated fat.

There are daily and weekly Smart Points so that you can track the amount of the food you are eating and what category of food you are eating. The Zero Points foods are having 0 Smart Point value and are selected because they are creating the basis for having a healthy and nutritious eating approach. They can also not be eaten in a bigger quantity than other foods. The WW Program is the best weight loss plan for sure.

Chapter 1: The principle of Weight Watchers

The principle of Weight Watchers is based on nutritional science and a program geared towards sustainable success. You are taught which foods and what food types are healthiest for you. This allows you to make healthier food decisions and no food is banned from the Weight Watchers program. This means it works alongside other diets and personal lifestyle choices. It also means that you don't feel limited or constricted in adopting this diet.

The goal is to lose weight through calorie reduction in a sustainable fashion through healthy eating. It also encourages the implementation of an exercise program and offers a local support group. You are invited to track your use and movements through activity tracker gadgets like the Fitbit. This will allow you to analyze what exercise you are doing and how it will work alongside your diet. The third principle is the support group where you will meet like-minded local people with this same aspiration has you.

You will also be guided by a success coach who has been on the same journey, has you? This is a vital part of Weight Watchers, and statistically, the more somebody attends the local meetings, the higher the likelihood of their success. It gives you the opportunity to tap into the wealth of knowledge available in the network and having a support group enhances your possibility of really succeeding long term.

Therefore, Weight Watchers operates on three key principles; healthy eating, a regular exercise program and a support group. There is also an online option where you don't attend meetings, but you have the opportunity to be part of an online community and network.

The program is very simple to follow and access to help readily available in the form of coaches, resources or the online or offline community. Firstly, you will have a confidential weigh in and set your ideal weight goal based upon your body mass index. If you are successful in this goal, you then begin a maintenance period for six weeks. This phase is to establish stability in your weight, and if successfully implemented you will become a lifetime member.

It's success factors are based upon a coach who has achieved success through the Weight Watchers program and a like-minded network which offers support, accountability, ideas and inspiration. This combined with the wealth of knowledge and tools online like the app, recipe ideas, expert chat facility, fitness videos and support network make you realize why it is the market leader in weight loss management.

Chapter 2: Food Cravings & How to Manage

That over-eating and food craving lead to weight gain, is a common knowledge. But, if you manage to overcome your food cravings, you can shed thousands of calories within no time. In this section, we explore the latest tricks by the researchers and experts as to how can you overcome your cravings.

Once you make up your mind to lose weight, you should try your best to avoid your triggers. For example, you crave for what you eat therefore, if you will switch to other things that you do not eat often, you will be able to weaken your old cravings. Studies say that this is the best way to eliminate your old cravings because the longer you avoid your trigger food, the lesser will be your craving for it. Ideally, you should switch to something healthy because in the end, you will possibly crave for the food items you have switched to. And, if you have switched to fresh fruits, it will be the real bonus.

Next trick is to destroy the temptation. If you have succumbed to a craving and bought your favorite junk food or any other trigger food and not feeling good while eating, destroy it. Do not throw it, but ruin it completely by running water over it. It will offer you the satisfaction that you have kicked your binge. However, you might feel bad that you have wasted money but just think if the junk food was not thrown away into the dustbin; it would have gone straight to your hips.

In order to eliminate your craving and clamp your appetite, drink two glasses of water and eat an ounce of nuts which includes walnuts, almonds, or peanuts. Within 20 minutes you will be able to overcome your craving completely. Moreover, nuts are quite good for your health, and if you eat them every day in an appropriate amount, you will definitely be amazed by the results.

Try switching to a skimmed latte, i.e. coffee, instead of going to your favorite restaurant and binging on unhealthy food. The caffeine it contains might not please your taste buds, but it can certainly save you the calories by satiating your craving.

Studies show that people in depression and stress tend to eat more. Therefore, it is important for you to learn how to deal with the stress. This way you will be able to shed lots of calories a day. However, this trick requires some practice. Deep breathing while relaxing or visualizing a tranquil scene on your own will be a good idea. You can divert to listening to powerful audios that teach progressive muscle relaxation.

When you are tired you feel like eating, therefore, it is the best time to take a power nap as it will reduce the exhaustion. The best thing you can do is shut the door, close your eyes and re-energize yourself.

After satisfactorily brushing your teeth in the morning, you wish not to eat anything for some time because you do not want to mess up the freshness. You can make the best use of this habit by brushing your teeth or by gargling with mouthwash. This is how you can control your food cravings, and you will definitely experience better results in the end.

Foods that are encouraged

The foods that are encouraged on the Weight Watchers plan are ones that are high in protein as well as those that have a lot of nutrients in them, such as fruits and vegetables. Low-fat dairy is also encouraged for muscle health, and whole grains are a good thing to add to the meal to keep you full and healthy.

Eating lots of healthy produce is a good foundation to start with. These have all the nutrients that you need to stay healthy and happy while losing weight. They are low in calories but can really fill you up more than some of the other options, so having them as the base for most of your meals and snacks can really help to fight off the cravings and keep you full.

Protein is really encouraged on the new Smart Points system. You can choose many types of protein including fish, turkey, and chicken. Be careful with some of the other options, like hamburger, that are higher in saturated fats and will make your points go up.

And of course, having some whole grains is always good to keep healthy. These have a lot of the B vitamins that your body needs to stay healthy, and it will ensure that you are able to feel full for longer while eating fewer calories. Keep in mind that there are differences between the whole grains and the processed grains; the processed grains are basically just glorified sugars and will be treated as such when using this program.

These are the food items that are going to keep you the healthiest. They have the most nutrition inside and will fill you up while you are still eating fewer calories in the long run. They taste good, and there are quite a few options that you can make out of them to really enjoy the diet. Mixing in a bit of the discouraged items on occasion can really help to mix things up and keep you healthy.

Foods that are discouraged

While you are allowed to consume any kind of food that you want when on the Weight Watchers diet, the points are set up to discourage the eating of some kinds of foods. For example, you may be allowed to have cookies on occasion, but do you really want to use up all your points on just a few of them during the day and have nothing else to eat? Eating something that is discouraged on the plan is not going to completely ruin your progress, you just need to be careful how you use these and only have them on occasion.

There are a number of foods that are discouraged on the Weight Watchers plan. These are mostly foods that are high in sugar and saturated fats, but some that are high in processed carbs are going to be discouraged as well. Things like cookies, ice cream, fried foods, freezer food selections (ones that are in the freezer at the store, not the freezer meals you make for yourself at home), candy, cake, most baked goods, and more. If they are high in calories, they are probably high in points so keep this in mind when selecting.

If you are uncertain about if a particular food is discouraged or not or you are curious about how many points it adds up to, make sure to check out the materials that you get from your meetings. This will help you to see how many points you would use up when it comes to eating that item that you want. Perhaps after seeing how many points that one item entails, you will decide that eating it is not worth all of that.

What about those drinks?

Another thing that you will need to consider when picking out what to eat during the day is what drinks you will be consuming. While options like green tea and water are not going to affect your points by much, there are some drinks that could take up as many of your points as a whole meal. These are mostly options like alcoholic and dessert drinks, and in reality, they are not giving you that many nutritional benefits for all the calories that are inside of them.

While you are allowed to have some of these drinks on occasion, you really need to watch the points and don't let them get away from you. Even regular fruit juices can be hard to fit within your points total because of all the sugar that is added to them and how Weight Watchers is discouraging items that have a lot of sugar.

If you don't want to ruin your points total for the day, it is best to stick with some simple options. Water and green tea are often the best because they contain few calories and won't take up all your points, but they provide the hydration that the body needs. Milk is a good option as well because it helps the body build strong bones and muscles. If you choose to have some juices, consider making some of your own so that you are able to avoid the extra sugars that are added to some of the store-bought varieties.

How to pick your meals

You are going to get a lot of say in your meals. Not only are you allowed a certain amount of points each day, but you are also only going to get some extra points that are going to be used for any of the cheats or those days that you are going to be up and moving a lot. Outside of staying within the points, you are going to be able to make the right decisions for your needs.

The best idea is to plan out meals that are healthy and keep you healthy all day long. Foods that are full of healthy vitamins and minerals are going to be one of the best choices that you can make when trying to lose weight. If you are able to stick mostly with these healthier meals that have all the nutrition that you need, you are all set for doing well on this diet.

There are going to be times when you are going to eat out with friends, go to a party, or some other event that is going to mess with your plans a bit. Luckily, you are able to go through and make changes to the points that you eat through the day so that you have some points left over while still getting a lot of the nutrition that you need for good health. Plus, when you get to the party, you will realize how many points you have left and may find that it is easier to avoid overeating because you don't want to ruin all your progress.

And this is part of why so many people have seen success when they are on Weight Watchers. There are some rules that will help you out, but there is a lot of flexibility that you need to make sure that you are able to fit it into your daily life. With all the great choices that you will be able to make using your new point system, you will find that it is easier to get the good nutrition that you need while also losing weight and staying healthy.

At each of the meetings that you attend, you will be given some more information that will help you to make the right food choices for your needs. You get to pick which foods that you want to eat, but keep in mind that sticking mainly with the foods that are in the encouraged category will ensure that you are getting the right nutrition into the day and that you are able to eat fewer calories without feeling hungry and deprived on the diet. Eating some of the discouraged foods is not a bad thing on occasion, you just need to make sure that you are keeping them to a minimum as much as possible.

Breakfast Recipes

Scrambled Eggs

Servings: 2

Ingredients

- 4 eggs
- 1/2 liter skimmed milk
- A pinch nutmeg
- 2 sprigs chopped parsley or chives
- Black pepper and salt, to taste

Direction

Beat eggs, add milk, then salt along with pepper.

Scrape off some nutmeg and cook slowly in the air fryer constantly stirring.

Garnish with some parsley or chives and serve immediately. Enjoy!

Chipotle Salsa

Servings: 4

Ingredients

- 8 cups roma tomatoes
- 4 cups sweet peppers, chopped
- 2 cups onions, minced
- 4 garlic cloves
- 1 hot pepper (such as jalepeno)
- 1 -2 tablespoon chipotle pepper, pureed
- 3/4 cup cider vinegar
- 1 tablespoon salt
- 1 tablespoon sugar
- 2 teaspoons paprika

- 16 ounces tomato paste
- 1/4 cup cilantro, copped

Directions

Blanch the tomatoes, remove the skin, and then chop. Measure 8 cups.

Mix all ingredients except the cilantro in a large pot and simmer until desired thickness is reached, approximately 1 to 1 1/2 hours. Add the cilantro just before you are ready to pour into jars.

Fill into hot, sterilized pint jars and top with hot, sterilized canning lids. We do not process in a canner and have never had a problem, but you may process in a hot-water-bath canner at this point for 20 minutes if you are concerned about food safety.

If you buy a half-bushel of tomatoes and adjust the rest of the ingredients accordingly you get about 6 batches and 36 pints.

Tofu Piccata

Servings: 4

Ingredients

- 1 large lemon, peeled and white pith removed
- 1/2 cup all-purpose flour
- 1 lb extra firm tofu, cut into 1/4 inch-thick slices
- salt & freshly ground black pepper
- 2 tablespoons olive oil
- 1/3 cup dry white wine
- 4 ounces white button mushrooms, thinly sliced
- 2 tablespoons capers, drained
- 2 tablespoons minced fresh parsley leaves
- 2 tablespoons butter or 2 tablespoons soy margarine (optional)

Directions

Preheat the oven to 275F.

Cut the lemon into very thin rounds, discarding the seeds, and set aside.

Drain tofu, wrap in paper towel, and press for about ten minutes (this will give your tofu a firmer texture).

Put the flour into a shallow bowl.

Season the tofu with salt and pepper and dredge in the flour, tapping off any excess.

Transfer the tofu slices to a platter and set aside.

Heat the oil in a large skillet over medium-high heat.

Add the tofu, in batches, and cook, turning once, until golden brown on both sides, about 2 minutes total.

Place the tofu slices on a baking sheet and keep warm in the oven.

Deglaze the skillet with the wine, scraping up any browned bits from the bottom.

Add the mushrooms and cook, stirring a few times, until slightly softened, about 2 minutes.

Stir in the lemon slices, capers, and parsley and simmer until hot.

Stir in the butter, if using, to enrich the sauce.

Arrange the tofu on a serving platter or individual plates.

Pour the sauce over the tofu and serve at once.

Thai Tofu and Squash Curry

Servings: 2

Ingredients

- 1 lb firm tofu or 1 lb extra firm tofu, drained

- 1 small butternut squash (about 2 lb/1 kg)

- 1 tablespoon vegetable oil

- 1 onion, sliced

- 2 garlic cloves, minced

- 2 teaspoons Thai red curry paste

- 14 ounces light coconut milk

- 1/2 cup vegetable stock

- 2 tablespoons soy sauce
- 1 tablespoon packed brown sugar
- 1 tablespoon fish sauce or 1 tablespoon soy sauce
- 1/2 teaspoon salt
- 1 sweet red pepper, thinly sliced
- 1/4 cup chopped fresh cilantro
- 2 tablespoons lime juice
- 2 tablespoons salted peanuts, chopped

Directions

Pat tofu dry with paper towels; cut into 3/4-inch (2 cm) cubes. Set aside.

Peel and seed squash; cut into 3/4-inch cubes to make 3 cups. Set aside.

In skillet, heat oil over medium heat; cook onion, garlic and curry paste, stirring occasionally, until onion is softened, about 5 minutes.

Add squash, coconut milk, stock, soy sauce, sugar, fish sauce and salt; bring to boil.

Reduce heat to low; partially cover and simmer until squash is almost tender, about 12 minutes.

Add red pepper; simmer for 5 minutes. Add tofu; simmer until heated through, about 2 minutes.

(Make-ahead: Let cool for 30 minutes. Refrigerate, uncovered, in airtight container until cold. Cover and refrigerate for up to 1 day. Reheat to continue.)

Stir in cilantro and lime juice; sprinkle with peanuts.

Banana Butter

Servings: 3

Ingredients

- 3 cups thoroughly mashed bananas (around 10-12ish)
- 1/4 cup fresh lemon juice
- 1/4 cup minced maraschino cherry

- 6 1/2 cups sugar
- 1 (6 ounce) bottle liquid pectin

Directions

Measure 3 cups mashed bananas into a large saucepan.

Add the lemon juice, cherries and sugar, mixing well.

Bring to a rolling boil and boil hard for 1 minute, stirring constantly.

Remove from heat and stir in the pectin.

Mix well.

Ladle into clean, hot sterile jars and seal.

Process in a boiling water bath for 10 minutes for pints.

Huckleberry Preserves

Servings: 6

Ingredients

- 4 1/2-5 cups huckleberries, washed
- 2/3 cup water
- 6 1/2 cups sugar
- 4 teaspoons fresh lemon zest
- 1/3 cup lemon juice
- 2 (1 3/4 ounce) packages dry pectin
- 1 tablespoon margarine

Directions

Put 2 1/2 cups huckleberries and 1/3 cup water in a blender with the lemon zest. Blend until pureed. Add balance of huckleberries and 1/3 cup water and puree.

In large stockpot, add pureed huckleberries, pectin, lemon juice and water.

Stir constantly. Bring to a rolling boil. A boil that cannot be stirred down.

Stir in Sugar. Stir until dissolved. Bring a full rolling boil. One that cannot be stirred down. Boil 1 minute exactly.

Stir in margarine.

Take off heat and skim any foam.

Pour in hot sterilized jars.

Wipe rims with a hot cloth and seal and band.

Put in a hot water bath for 15 minutes.

Take out on a toweled counter. Keep away from drafts until they seal.

Tuna Omelet

Servings: 4

Ingredients

- 2 anchovy fillets
- 8 eggs
- 200 g canned tuna (fat-free)
- 1 tbsp. chopped parsley
- Black pepper, to taste

Direction

Cut anchovies into thin strips.

Beat eggs, adding anchovies and tuna.

Season with parsley and black pepper.

Cook the omelet in a lightly oiled air fryer pan at medium temperature.

Serve immediately. Enjoy!

Yellow Pear Tomato Preserves

Servings: 3

Ingredients

- 8 cups yellow pear tomatoes
- 1 lemon
- 3 cups sugar

- 1 teaspoon salt
- 4 tablespoons gingerroot or 4 tablespoons thinly sliced candied ginger

Directions

Wash& dry tomatoes.

Cut a thin slice from blossom end and press out seeds and discard.

Combine tomatoes, sugar& salt, simmer until sugar is dissolved.

Boil for about 40 minutes.

Add thinly sliced lemon and minced or sliced ginger.

Boil about 10 minutes longer.

Pour into hot jars and seal at once

Preserved Grape Leaves

Servings: 4

Ingredients

- 1 quart young spring grape leaves, about stem end removed
- 2 teaspoons kosher salt, in
- 1 quart water
- 1 cup fresh lemon juice or 2 1/2 teaspoons citric acid
- 1 quart water

Directions

Bring salted water to a boil.

Add washed grape leaves and blanch for 30 seconds.

Drain.

Stack them on each other into 2 piles then form into loose rolls and stand each roll up in 2 pint canning jars.

Add lemon juice or citric acid to the second quart of water and bring to a boil.

Fill jars within 1/2 inch of top with the hot mixture.

Seal.

Process in a boiling water bath for 15 minutes.

Green Tomato Preserves

Servings: 4

Ingredients

- 4 lbs. green tomatoes
- 1 lemon, juice of
- 5 cups sugar
- 1/8 cup crystallized ginger to 1/4 cup crystallized ginger (optional)

Directions

Wash the tomatoes, core and cut into chunks; place in a large canning kettle.

Add the lemon juice and sugar, bring to a boil and continue boiling until syrup is thick.

Ladle into hot sterilized jars and process in water bath as recommended in your area

Vanilla Fig Preserves

Servings: 4

Ingredients

- 3 1/2 cups sugar
- 1 vanilla pod, split
- 1 large lemon, juice and zest , meat diced
- 2 lbs. fresh figs, quartered
- 1/4 cup Limon cello or 1/4 cup Grand Marnier

Directions

In a large pot place sugar, vanilla pod and the seeds into the figs, lemon juice, zest and meat of lemon. Do squeeze any juice from the peels into the sugar and figs.

Stir to release juices it will be thick. Simmer over low heat stirring not to burn. Juices will come and when it does raise heat to high stirring most of the time.

When it hits a rolling boil for 15 minutes all the time stirring add liquor cook 1 minute.

Pour into sterile jars and process 10 minutes.

Optional for those that like it smoother without chunks you can blend thee figs before adding to sugar or use an immersion blender while cooking

Fig Preserves

Servings: 4

Ingredients

- 2 lbs. figs, unpeeled
- 3 cups granulated sugar
- 1 cup water
- 1/2 lemon, sliced thin

Directions

Wash figs gently in cold water.

Place in a large bowl, fill with cool water and soak for 20 minutes.

Make syrup by boiling the sugar and water together in a large saucepan.

When syrup is clear and just thick, around 15 minutes add figs and lemon slices.

Bring to a boil over high heat.

Boil hard 1 minute.

Lower heat and simmer for 30 minutes.

Remove from heat.

Carefully pour into a blender and pulse to grind figs and lemon slices.

You may want to cook down for 10 or 15 more minutes to desired thickness.

Ladle into clean hot sterile jars and process in a boiling water bath for 10 minutes.

Fried Tofu

Servings: 4

Ingredients

- 1 (350 g) package extra firm tofu
- 3 tablespoons tamari or 3 tablespoons soya sauce
- 1/4 cup Red Star nutritional yeast
- 1 teaspoon seasoning (EG Tony Chachere's, Mrs Dash or mix your own combination)
- 1 tablespoon olive oil, to lightly grease a skillet (or other veggie oil)

Directions

Lightly grease a non-stick pan with oil.

Put tamari (soy sauce) in a bowl.

In another bowl mix yeast and spices.

Slice tofu into 1/4-inch slices.

Dip tofu in the tamari and then in the yeast mixture.

Fry until golden; flip and brown the other side.

Add a bit of oil if necessary.

Japanese Pickled Ginger

Servings: 3

Ingredients

- 1 1/2 cups peeled gingerroot, sliced into 2 x 1/8 inch slivers
- 1 1/4 cups rice vinegar
- 1 teaspoon honey
- 1 teaspoon red miso

Directions

Soak ginger slivers in ice water, covered for 12 hours.

Drain.

In a small stainless or enamel saucepan combine vinegar, honey and miso.

Bring to a boil.

Pack drained ginger into 2 half pint jars.

Pour hot liquid over ginger, leaving 1/2 inch head space.

Seal and process in a boiling water bath for 10 minutes at altitudes up to 1000 feet.

See altitude chart for higher altitudes

Pear Preserves

Servings: 2

Ingredients

- 4 lbs. pears (whole, halved or quartered)
- 4 cups water
- 4 cups sugar
- 2 lemons, sliced thin

Directions

Boil 2 cups sugar and 2 cups water together for 15 minutes.

Add pears and sliced lemon and cook 15 minutes.

Add remaining sugar and water and cook until pears are clear and transparent and syrup is thick.

Pack into clean hot jars and seal at once.

Preserved Lemons

Servings: 3

Ingredients

- 2 1/2-3 lbs. lemons (10 to 12)
- 2/3 cup coarse salt
- 1/4 cup olive oil

Directions

Blanch 6 lemons in boiling water 5 minutes.

When cool enough to handle, cut lemons into 8 wedges each and discard seeds.

Toss with salt in a bowl and pack into jar.

Squeeze enough juice from remaining lemons to measure 1 cup.

Add enough juice to cover lemons and cover jar with lid.

Let stand at room temperature, shaking gently once a day, 5 days.

Add oil and chill.

Preserved lemons keep, chilled, up to 1 year.

Award Winning Pineapple Preserves

Servings: 4

Ingredients

- 20 ounces crushed pineapple in juice
- 2 cups granulated sugar

Directions

Bring pineapple and sugar to a boil in a large saucepan and cook 20 minutes, stirring constantly until thickened or until the temperature reaches 220F on a thermometer (this is the jelling stage at sea level).

Pour immediately into hot sterilized jars; wipe rims with a clean cloth, place lids and screw on bands fingertip-tight.

Process jars in a water-bath canner for 5 minutes.

Place jars on a clean towel.

Cover with towel to prevent drafts and let cool undisturbed for 24 hours.

Frozen Bell Peppers

Servings: 5

Ingredients

- fresh bell pepper, any and all colors
- water, for washing

Directions

Clean peppers, removing membrane and seeds; wash and pat dry.

Rough chop. (You can chop to whatever size you need when you use them.).

Place in zip top bag, removing as much air as possible, or vacuum pack.

Freeze.

Use these in chili recipes, soups or stews, anywhere you want the flavor and color of fresh bell peppers!

Mains Meals

Slow Cook Beef Lasagna

Servings: 2

Ingredients

- Parmesan cheese (.5 cups shredded)

- Lasagna noodles (6)

- Mozzarella cheese (1.5 cups shredded)

- Ricotta cheese (1 cup)

- Red pepper flakes (.25 tsp.)

- Basil (.5 tsp. dried)

- Oregano (1 tsp. dried)

- Salt (1 tsp.)

- Tomato sauce (15 oz.)

- Tomato (28 oz. crushed)

- Garlic (1 clove minced)

- Onion (1 chopped)

- Ground beef (1 lb.)

DIRECTIONS

Place a skillet on the stove on top of a burner set to a high/medium heat before adding in the garlic, onion and beef and letting the beef brown.

Add in the red pepper flakes, basil, oregano, salt, tomato sauce and crushed tomatoes and let the results simmer 5 minutes.

Combine the mozzarella and the ricotta cheese.

Add .3 of the total sauce from the skillet and add it to the slow cooker. Place 3 noodles on top of the sauce, followed by cheese mixture. Create three layers total.

Cover the slow cooker and let it cook on a low heat for 6 hours.

Lobster Tails with Brussels Sprouts

Servings: 6

Ingredients:

For cooking:

- Water

For lobster tails:

- 2 lbs lobster tails
- 1 tsp sea salt
- 1 tsp Italian seasoning
- 1 tsp dried rosemary, ground

For Brussels sprouts:

- 1 cup Brussels sprouts, chopped
- 2 tsp butter
- ½ tsp dried thyme, ground
- 2 garlic cloves, minced
- ¼ tsp salt

Directions:

Plug in the Instant Pot and pour 1 cup of water in the stainless-steel insert. Position a trivet on the bottom and set aside.

Place the lobster tails in the steam basket and sprinkle with salt, Italian seasoning, and rosemary. Set the basket on top of a trivet and close the lid.

Adjust the steam release handle and press the Manual button. Set the timer for 3 minutes and cook on High pressure.

When you hear the cookers end signal, release the pressure naturally.

Meanwhile, melt the butter in a small saucepan over medium-high heat. Add Brussels sprouts and sprinkle with some salt, thyme, and garlic. Cook for 4-5 minutes, or until crispy on the edges. Remove from the heat.

Serve lobster tails with Brussels sprouts and enjoy!

Bacon Chops

Servings: 2

Ingredients

- 2 pork chops (I prefer bone-in, but boneless chops work great as well)
- 1 bag shredded brussels sprouts
- 4 slices of bacon
- Worcestershire sauce
- Lemon juice (optional)

Directions:

Place the pork chops on a baking sheet with the Worcestershire sauce inside a preheated grill for 5 minutes.

Turnover and cook for another 5 minutes. Put to the side when done.

Cook the chopped bacon in a large pan until browned. Add the shredded brussels sprouts and cook together.

Stir the brussels sprouts with the bacon and grease and cook for 5 minutes until the bacon is crisp.

Lemon Herb Baked Salmon

Servings: 8

Ingredients

- 1 salmon fillet 3-4lbs
- salt & pepper
- 1 lemon divided
- 2 tablespoons butter melted

Topping

- ¾ cup Panko bread crumbs
- 3 tablespoons butter melted
- 2 tablespoons parmesan cheese shredded
- 1 tablespoon fresh dill minced

- zest from one lemon
- 2 tablespoons fresh parsley minced
- 3 cloves garlic minced

Directions

1. Preheat the oven to 400oF

2. Put all ingredients together in a small bowl.

3. Streak a pan with foil and spray with cooking spray.

4. Put salmon on the pan and brush with melted butter. Season with salt and pepper and crush ½

of the lemon over top.

5. Sprinkle crumb mixture over salmon. Bake exposed for 15 minutes or until salmon flakes easily and is cooked.

Note

Salmon cooking time will vary based on thinness or thickness. Your salmon should flake easily with a fork.

White Cheddar Broccoli Mac & Cheese:

Servings: 1

Ingredients:

- 1/2 cups milk
- 2 egg whites
- 2 teaspoons cornstarch or custard starch
- 1/8 teaspoon nutmeg
- 1 cup ground white cheddar
- 1 little head of broccoli, cut into nibble measured florets
- 2 cups dry, entire wheat pasta

DIRECTIONS

Whisk together the milk, egg whites and cornstarch in the cooker embeds. Make certain to whisk well.

Blend in the ground cheddar, broccoli and pasta shells.

Cook on low for 1-1/2 to 2 hours.

After the main hour, mix the sustenance on a semi-consistent premise.

This will do two things. It will permit the pasta to cook equally.

It will likewise permit you to watch out for the pasta and see when it's set.

Each moderate cooker is distinctive, so the planning for this formula might be marginally unique on this for you.

Pasta goes from "cooked" to "mush" rapidly.

So make certain to continue mixing every so often to watch out for things.

Meatballs

Servings: 6

Ingredients

- 1 lb ground beef (or ½ lb beef, ½ lb pork)
- ½ cup grated parmesan cheese
- 1 tbsp minced garlic (or paste)
- ½ cup mozzarella cheese
- 1 tsp freshly ground pepper

Directions:

Preheat your oven to 400°F/200°C.

In a bowl, mix all the ingredients together.

Roll the meat mixture into 5 generous meatballs.

Bake inside your oven at 170°F/80°C for about 18 minutes.

Serve with sauce!

Instant Pot Queso Chicken

Servings: 5

Ingredients:

- 2 lb chicken tenderloin (un-skinned and boneless)
- 10 ounces of canned tomatoes
- ½ cup of chicken bone broth
- 1, ½ cup of shredded Cheese (Monterey Jack)
- One tablespoon of taco seasonings
- 4 oz of cream cheese
- Salt and pepper, as you like

Directions

Mix the chicken with salt, pepper and taco seasoning and put it into the instant pot.

Now add bone broth and canned tomatoes over the chicken and layer it with cream cheese. Lock the pot.

Prepare chicken on high pressure/manual method for 15 minutes.

Release the steam release naturally for ten minutes, then quick release the remaining steam.

Open the pot and mix until well-combined. Now add monetary jack cheese and continue stirring until the cheese is fully melted.

Your chicken is ready, enjoy it with cauliflower rice or a bowl of keto salad.

Tuscan-Style Tuna Salad

Servings: 4

Ingredients

- 2 6-ounce cans chunk light tuna, drained.
- ¼ teaspoon salt
- 10 cherry tomatoes
- 2 tablespoons lemon juice

- 4 scallions, trimmed and sliced
- 2 tablespoons extra-virgin olive oil
- 15-ounce can small white beans
- Freshly ground pepper

Directions

1. Mix tuna, beans, scallions, tomatoes, juice, oil, lemon, pepper, and salt in a medium bowl. Stir gently. Refrigerate until ready to serve.

Mackerel in Tartar Sauce

Servings: 8

Ingredients:

For cooking:

- Nonstick cooking spray

For mackerel:

- 2 lbs mackerel fillets, thinly sliced
- 2 tbsp fresh lemon juice
- 3 tsp olive oil
- 1 tsp sea salt
- ½ tsp dried thyme, ground

For tartar sauce:

- 2 tbsp pickles, finely chopped
- 1 tbsp capers, finely chopped
- 1 tbsp mayonnaise, fat-free
- ¼ tsp sugar
- 1 tsp onion powder
- ¼ tsp garlic powder
- ½ tsp dried dill, ground

Directions:

In a medium-sized mixing bowl, combine mayonnaise, sugar, onion, powder, garlic powder, and dried dill. Mix until combined and then add pickles and capers. Mix again and cover with a lid. Refrigerate til later.

Rinse the fish fillets under cold running water. Pat dry with a kitchen paper and place in a large bowl. Drizzle with lemon juice and olive oil. Sprinkle with salt and dried thyme. Gently rub with your hands to coat all. Refrigerate for 20 minutes before cooking.

Grease the stainless-steel insert of your Instant Pot with some cooking spray. Press the Sauté button and add fillets. Cook for 2-3 minutes on each side.

Optionally, add 1 cup of water and close the lid. Adjust the steam release handle and press the Manual button. Set the timer for 3 minutes and cook on High pressure.

When done, perform a quick pressure release and open the pot.

Transfer the fish to a serving plate and drizzle with tartar sauce. Enjoy!

Poached Salmon with Creamy Piccata Sauce

Servings: 4

Ingredients

- 1 pound center-cut salmon fillet, skinned and cut into 4 portions

- 2 tablespoons lemon juice

- 2 teaspoons extra-virgin olive oil

- ¼ cup reduced-fat sour cream

- 1 large shallot, minced

- 1 cup dry white wine, divided

- 1 tablespoon chopped fresh dill

- 4 teaspoons capers, rinsed

- ¼ teaspoon salt

Directions

1. Place salmon in a wide skillet and add ½ cup wine and sufficient water to just cover the salmon. Bring it to boil over high-temperature heat. Reduce to a simmer, turn the salmon over, cover and cook for 5 minutes and then remove from the heat.

2. In the meantime, heat oil in a medium skillet over moderate heat. Add shallot and cook, stirring, until scented, about 30 seconds. Add the remaining ½ cup wine; boil until slightly condensed, about 1 minute. Stir in lemon juice and capers; cook 1 minute more. Remove from the heat; stir in sour cream and salt. To serve, top the salmon with the sauce and relish with dill.

Buffalo Chicken Meat Balls

Servings: 6

Ingredients:

- 1.5 lb ground chicken

- Two garlic cloves (minced)

- Two green onions (sliced)

- ¾ cup of almond meal

- Six tablespoons of hot sauce

- Two tablespoon ghee

- Four tablespoons of butter

- Salt, as you like

- Green onion (chopped)

Directions

Take a large bowl and mix chicken, chopped green onions, garlic, salt and almond meal in it. Mix it well

Grease your hand with butter and make 1-inch wide, chicken meatball.

Take out your Instant Pot and select the sauté option.

Now add the meatballs in the pot and brown them well. (Work in batches)

Mix hot sauce and butter and melt it in the pan or microwave it. It's your buffalo sauce.

Now pour the sauce over the meatballs and put all the meatballs back in the instant pot and close the lid.

Cook the meatballs for 20 minutes on the high-pressure setting.

Allow the pressure to release quickly.

Your meatballs are ready enjoy with zoodles or cauliflower rice.

Roast Beef Lettuce Wraps

Servings: 4

Ingredients

- 8 large iceberg lettuce leaves
- 8 oz (8 slices) rare roast beef
- ½ cup homemade mayonnaise
- 8 slices provolone cheese
- 1 cup baby spinach

Directions:

Wash the lettuce leaves and sake them dry. Try not to rip them.

Place 1 slice of roast beef inside each wrap.

Smother 1 tablespoon of mayonnaise on top of each piece of roast beef.

Top the mayonnaise with 1 slice of provolone cheese and 1 cup of baby spinach.

Roll the lettuce up around the toppings.

Serve & enjoy!

Easy Keto Chicken Taco Meat Recipe

Servings: 4

Ingredients:

- Four chicken breasts
- One onion (sliced)
- Four bell peppers (sliced)
- Three tablespoon ghee
- Two tablespoons of paprika
- Two tablespoons of garlic powder
- One tablespoon of cumin powder

- One teaspoon of chili powder

- Salt and pepper, as you like

Directions:

Turn on your instant pot and add all the ingredients into it.

Prepare the taco meat for 25 minutes on high pressure/manual mode. Allow the steam to release naturally.

Take out the chicken breast from the instant pot, and shred into pieces.

Your easy keto chicken is ready. Serve it with lettuce, guacamole or kale leaves.

Instant Pot Café Rio Chicken

Servings: 4

Ingredients:

- ¼ cup of chicken broth

- 1 cup of Italian dressing

- Two and ½ lbs of chicken thighs and two and ½ lb f chicken breasts

- One tablespoon of cumin

- One tablespoon of chili powder

- Salt, as you like

- One tablespoon of garlic powder

Directions

Include the chicken stock and Italian dressing to the pot. Include the remainder of the fixings. Close the pot and turn the valve to "fixing." Push manual and cook for 17 minutes.

At the point when the weight cooker signals, let the steam discharge normally for 5 minutes and afterward quickly release it.

Move the chicken to a cutting board and shred and afterward include the chicken over into sauce inside the Instant Pot. Mix well and serve the chicken.

You may need to salt and pepper to taste.

Chicken in a Blanket

Servings: 3

Ingredients

- 3 boneless chicken breasts
- 1 package bacon
- 1 8-oz package cream cheese
- 3 jalapeno peppers
- Salt, pepper, garlic powder or other seasonings

Directions:

Cut the chicken breast in half lengthwise to create two pieces.

Cut the jalapenos in half lengthwise and remove the seeds.

Dress each breast with a half-inch slice of cream cheese and half a slice of jalapeno. Sprinkle with garlic powder, salt and pepper.

Roll the chicken and wrap 2 to 3 pieces of bacon around it—secure with toothpicks.

Bake in a preheated 375°F/190°C oven for 50 minutes.

Serve!

Beef Casserole

Servings: 6

Ingredients

- ½ lb ground beef
- ½ cup chopped onion
- ½ bag coleslaw mix
- 1-1/2 cups tomato sauce
- 1 tbsp lemon juice

Directions:

In a skillet, cook the ground beef until browned and to the side.

Mix in the onion and cabbage to the skillet and sauté until soft.

Add the ground beef back in along with the tomato sauce and lemon juice.

Bring the mixture to a boil, then cover and simmer for 30 minutes.

Enjoy!

Easy Zoodles & Turkey Balls

Servings: 2

Ingredients

- 1 zucchini, cut into spirals

- 1 can vodka pasta sauce

- 1 package frozen Armour Turkey meatballs

Directions:

Cook the meatballs and sauce on a high heat for 25 minutes, stirring occasionally.

Wash the zucchini and put through a vegetable spiral maker.

Boil the water and blanch the raw zoodles for 60 seconds. Remove and drain.

Combine the zoodles and prepared saucy meatballs.

Serve!

Lemon Tuna with Herbs

Servings: 4

Ingredients:

For cooking:

- 2 tsp olive oil

For lemon tuna:

- 1 lb tuna fillets, cut into bite-sized pieces

- 1 whole lemon, thinly sliced

- 1 medium-sized red bell pepper, chopped

- 1 tbsp fresh parsley, finely chopped

- ½ tsp sea salt
- ¼ tsp black pepper, ground

Herbs:

1 fresh rosemary sprig

1 tsp fresh thyme, finely chopped

1 tsp fresh sage, finely chopped

Directions:

Grease the stainless steel insert of your Instant Pot with some cooking spray. Add chopped tuna and sprinkle with some salt and pepper. Cook for 1 minute on each side and then add bell pepper. Stir-fry for 2-3 minutes.

Now, pour 1 cup of water and add all the remaining ingredients and herbs. Stir once and securely lock the lid.

Set the steam release handle and press the Manual button. Set the timer for 2 minutes and cook on High pressure.

When you hear the cookers end signal, perform a quick pressure release by moving the valve to the Venting position. Open the pot and drain the tuna and pepper.

Transfer to a serving plate and garnish with some fresh lemon. Enjoy!

Instant Pot Chicken Breasts

Servings: 3

Ingredients:

- Three chicken breasts (un-skinned and boneless)
- One tablespoon of avocado oil or coconut oil
- 1/8 teaspoon of oregano (dried)
- ¼ teaspoon of garlic powder
- 1/8 teaspoon of basil (dried)
- salt and pepper, as you like
- 1 cup of water

Directions

Marinate chicken breasts with seasonings well.

Set your instant pot to the highest function of sautéing settings and let it heat.

Add oil into the heated pot and put the chicken breast in it.

Let the chicken cooks for 4 minutes on each side then take out the chicken from the pot.

Pour water into the pot and set the steamer rack in it.

Carefully place the chicken on the trivet and lock the lid. Let it cook for 5 minutes on high-pressure method and manual setting.

Release the steam release naturally for five minutes, then quick release the remaining steam.

Your dish is ready, serve hot and enjoy.

Mediterranean Chicken

Servings: 4

Ingredients:

- 3 pound of chicken thighs
- Three garlic cloves (sliced)
- One tablespoon of lemon juice
- 1 cup of Greek yoghurt (whole milk)
- One teaspoon lemon zest
- 1 cup of kalamata olives
- 1, ½ teaspoon of oregano (dried)
- Two tablespoon of mint leaves (fresh and hashed)
- ¼ cup parsley (fresh and hashed)
- One tablespoon of olive oil
- Two tablespoon capers
- Two tablespoons of white wine vinegar
- Salt and pepper, as you like

Directions

Mix the chicken with salt and pepper in a bowl. Put the bowl away.

Turn on your multi pressure cooker, i.e. instant pot and turn on saute setting. Allow the pot to heat thoroughly.

Add oil and chicken in the pot and cook it from both sides until its adequately browned. (work in batches, so the chicken is properly cooked)

Take out the chicken and add garlic in the pot, sauté until translucent. Now add crepes, olives oregano, and water in the pot and stir it well until combines.

Turn off the instant pot and put the steamer rack or trivet inside the pot over the olive mixture. Put the chicken carefully on the trivet and lock the lid. Cook the chicken for 10 minutes at manual/ high pressure.

Release the steam quickly.

Prepare yoghurt sauce by mixing parsley, mint, zest, salt, pepper, and lemon juice in the yoghurt. Mix it well.

Take out the chicken from the pot and pour the olive mixture on it with the help of a spoon.

Select the sauté setting and simmer the sauce until it is slightly thick.

Your chicken is ready. Enjoy it with the yoghurt sauce.

Low-Carb Creamy Garlic Tuscan Chicken Thigh

Servings: 4

Ingredients:

- Four chicken thigh pieces

- One teaspoon olive oil

- One cup bone broth (low sodium)

- ¼ cup tomatoes (sun-dried)

- Three garlic cloves (chopped)

- 2, ½ cup spinach (fresh)

- 4 ounces of cream cheese

- Two teaspoons of Italian seasoning

- ¼ cup parmesan cheese (sharply grated)

- 1 cup of almond milk (unsweetened)

- One tablespoon of chicken seasoning

- ½ teaspoon xanthan gum

- Two tablespoons of heavy whipping cream

- Salt and pepper, as you like

Directions

Cover the chicken with salt, pepper, and Italian seasoning and make sure the chicken is pat dry.

Turn on your instant pot and select the saute option. Add oil and marinate the chicken in it. Cook the chicken until it's appropriately browned from both sides.

Then add broth, chicken seasoning, and milk into the pot. Lock the lid and cook it on high pressure for 14 minutes.

Release the steam quickly.

Unlock the lid and take the chicken out from the pot. Now add cream cheese, tomatoes, garlic, parmesan cheese, and spinach in the instant pot and sauté it spinach is wilted, and cheese is fully melted.

Add the xanthan gum to thick the sauce.

Pour the sauce over the chicken. Enjoy.

Delicious Mexican Meatloaf

Servings: 1

Ingredients:

For Meatloaf:

- 2 tablespoons olive oil

- 1 onion, slashed

- 1 jalapeño, minced

- 1 clove garlic, minced

- 1 pound ground hamburger

- 1 teaspoon ground cumin

- 1/4 teaspoon cayenne pepper

- 1/2 teaspoon ocean salt

- 1/4 teaspoon dark pepper

- 1/2 cup moved oats, coarsely ground in a sustenance processor

- 1 egg

For Coat:

- 1 cup diced tomatoes in juice

- 1 clove garlic, minced

- 1 tablespoon nectar

- 1 tablespoon lime juice

- 1 canned chipotle stew in adobo sauce

- 1/4 teaspoon Kosher salt

DIRECTIONS

Warm a skillet over medium warmth. Include the olive oil, onions, and jalapeño.

Cook until delicate and include the garlic. Cook for 1 moment and add to a huge bowl.

Blend in the hamburger and seasonings and blend well. At the point when the blend is marginally cool, include the oats and egg.

Shape the blend into a round chunk and exchange to a moderate cooker pot. Cover and cook on low, for 6 hours.

Before serving, make the coating by consolidating the greater part of the fixings in a little pan. Heat until it starts boiling.

Cook for 5 minutes and exchange to a blender. Mix until smooth.

Spoon the meatloaf before serving.

Buffalo Chicken Salad

Servings: 1

Ingredients

- 3 cups salad of your choice
- 1 chicken breast
- 1/2 cup shredded cheese of your choice
- Buffalo wing sauce of your choice
- Ranch or blue cheese dressing

Directions:

Preheat your oven to 400°F/200°C.

Douse the chicken breast in the buffalo wing sauce and bake for 25 minutes. In the last 5 minutes, throw the cheese on the wings until it melts.

When cooked, remove from the oven and slice into pieces.

Place on a bed of lettuce.

Pour the salad dressing of your choice on top.

Serve!

Buffalo Turkey Meatballs:

Servings: 3

Ingredients:

For Meatballs

- 1/4 cup non-fat milk
- 2 cuts entire wheat sandwich bread
- 14 ounces lean, ground chicken or turkey
- 1 teaspoon salt, partitioned
- 1/4 teaspoon pepper
- 1/4 teaspoon cayenne pepper
- 1/2 cup Parmesan cheddar

- 1 egg

For Sauce

- 2 teaspoons olive oil
- 1 little sweet onions, diced
- 2 cloves garlic, minced
- 1 cup hot sauce
- 1 (4 ounces) can dice green chilies
- 1/2 cup nectar
- 1 teaspoon bean stew powder
- 1 teaspoon paprika
- 1/4 teaspoon cayenne pepper
- 1/2 teaspoon dark pepper
- 1 teaspoon genuine or ocean salt

DIRECTIONS

Preheat stove to 450 degrees and line a preparing sheet with aluminum thwart.

In a little bowl, absorb the bread the milk. In an extensive bowl, blend the chicken or turkey, Parmesan, 1/2 teaspoon salt, pepper, egg, and the bread absorbed milk.

Blend well until it gets to be distinctly conservative.

Get about a tablespoon of the meat then come in the middle of your palms to make the meatballs—we made them utilizing a 1" scoop.

Put them on the heating sheet. Cook for 6 minutes.

For the sauce, warm the olive oil on medium-low. Include the onions and garlic and sauté until onions are translucent.

Include the onions, garlic, and every one of extra fixings to a bowl and race until smooth.

Add enough meatballs to cover the base of the moderate cooker, and then pour half of the sauce.

Include the rest of the meatballs and pour whatever remains of the sauce.

Cover and cook on low 2-4 hours, or until meatballs are cooked through.

Instant Pot Chicken Vindaloo

Servings: 4

Ingredients:

- Five garlic cloves

- 1 cup of onions (diced)

- One tablespoon of oil

- Three slices of ginger (minced)

- 1 cup of tomato (chopped)

- ¼ cup of white vinegar

- One teaspoon of paprika (smoked)

- One teaspoon of garam masala

- ½ teaspoon of coriander

- Two teaspoons of cayenne pepper

- 1 pound of chicken thighs (un-skinned and boneless)

- ½ teaspoon of turmeric

- ¼ cup of water

Directions

In a microwave-safe bowl, heat the garlic, onions, ginger, and oil for 5 - 7 minutes until the vegetables are sautéed on the edges.

Empty veggies into a blender and add all other ingredients aside from turmeric, chicken, and water. Mix to combine well.

Spot chicken in a bowl, and coat with the zest and vegetable blend. Mix well to cover the chicken. Wash out the blender bowl with the 1/4 cup water and pour that over the chicken also. Blend.

Include turmeric and marinate for 30 mins to 8 hours.

Empty the chicken and marinate into your Instant Pot.

Cook on High Pressure for 5 minutes, and enable pressure to discharge normally for 10 minutes. Release remaining pressure quickly.

Contingent upon your chicken and how much water it releases, you may need to expel the chicken pieces and dissipate a portion of the water by utilizing the Sauté capacity to cook the sauce down.

Sausage Balls

Servings: 6

Ingredients

- 12 oz Jimmy Dean's Sausage

- 6 oz. shredded cheddar cheese

- 10 cubes cheddar (optional)

Directions:

Mix the shredded cheese and sausage.

Divide the mixture into 12 equal parts to be stuffed.

Add a cube of cheese to the center of the sausage and roll into balls.

Fry at 375°F/190°C until crisp.

Serve!

Chicken with Mushroom Gravy:

Servings: 4

Ingredients:

- 1 tablespoon additional virgin olive oil

- 4 cuts without nitrate bacon, diced (we utilized turkey bacon)

- 4 boneless, skinless lean chicken bosom filets

- 16 ounces cut cremini mushrooms

- 1 yellow onion daintily cut into rings

- 2 cloves garlic, minced

- 1/2 teaspoon dark pepper

- 1 teaspoon legitimate or ocean salt

- 1/4 cup new level leaf parsley, slashed

- 1/2 cups chicken soup, low-sodium, sans fat

- 2 tablespoons flour

DIRECTIONS

Add oil to an extensive skillet, swing to medium-high warmth, include diced bacon and cook until fresh.

Exchange to a plate with a paper towel on it. Add chicken to the skillet and burn chicken on both sides just until brilliant cocoa.

Remove and put on a paper towel.

Diminish warmth to medium-low, add onion to a similar skillet, and sauté until delicate, around 4 minutes.

Add chicken to a moderate cooker, and then cover with diced bacon, onion, and remaining ingredients, aside from the flour.

Wrap and roast on low temperature for 3 to 4 hours, or on high temperature for 1 to 3 hours, or until the chicken is done and effectively drops with a fork.

Expel chicken from moderate cooker and put aside. Add flour to a moderate cooker and race until smooth.

Return chicken to moderate cooker and keep cooking until sauce is thick 10-15 minutes.

When you add the onion to the skillet, pour in around a 1/4 cup soup to deglaze the dish and get every one of the bits on the base of the container from the chicken and afterward add to the moderate cooker.

Slow cooker Spinach Enchiladas

Servings: 8

Ingredients:

- 1 package of thawed frozen spinach

- 1 cup of corn

- 2 jars salsa Verde

- 2 cups reduced fat sharp cheddar, shredded up

- 1 t ground cumin and coriander

- 1 t chili powder

- 1 can of black beans, drained and rinsed out

- 8 whole wheat tortillas

- ½ cup sour cream

- Juice from a lime

Directions

Squeeze water from spinach and then mash the black beans with a fork. Do about half of these, and then add in the rest of the ingredients besides the tortillas and the salsa

Put a jar of the salsa into the bottom of your slow cooker and then put the bean and spinach mixture into this, rolling it up and putting it seam-side down. Lay them on a single layer to make it easier with removing

Top it with salsa and more shredded cheese

Cook it for about 3 hours and top with the sour cream, cilantro, onions, and jalapenos, using other toppings of choice.

Orange Chicken

Servings: 6

Ingredients:

- 2 lb chicken breasts (un-skinned and cubed)

- 75 ml of orange juice (sugar-free and chunk free)

- One teaspoon dark brown sugar

- Three tablespoon tamari sauce

- One tablespoon of apple cider vinegar

- ½ teaspoon ginger (grated)

- ½ teaspoon garlic (minced)

- ¼ teaspoon chili (flaked)

- 1, ½ tablespoon of cornflour

- One teaspoon sesame oil
- Salt, as you like

Directions

Add chicken and all other ingredients into the bowl and mix them well. Put the bowl away.

Open your instant port and set the vent of the pot to sealing. Add chicken in the instant pot.

Prepare the chicken on high-pressure mode for 5 minutes.

When timer beeps, let the steam release naturally for 10 minutes, then quick release the remaining steam.

Mix cornflour in 1 tablespoon of water to make the paste, make sure it is lump-free.

Turn on the sauté setting and pour the paste over the chicken, mix it well and saute it for 3 minutes, until its thick.

Your chicken is ready to garnish with sesame seed and spring onion.

Shrimps in Honey Mirin Sauce

Servings: 4

Ingredients:

For cooking:

- 1 cup fish stock

For shrimps:

- 1 lb shrimps, peeled and deveined
- 1 tbsp spring onions, finely chopped

For honey wasabi sauce:

- 1 tbsp honey
- 2 tbsp mirin
- ½ tsp wasabi paste
- 1 tbsp soy sauce, low-sodium

- 1 tsp balsamic vinaigrette

- ½ tsp salt

- ½ tsp black pepper, ground

Directions:

Plug in the Instant Pot and pour in the fish stock. Add shrimps and securely lock the lid. Set the steam release handle by moving the valve to the Sealing position. Press the Manual button and set the timer for 1 minute. Cook on High pressure.

When you hear the cookers end signal, release the pressure naturally.

Meanwhile, combine all sauce ingredients in a small bowl. Mix until combined.

Open the pot and remove the shrimps using a slotted spoon. Reserve the liquid.

Press the Sauté button and pour in the sauce. Bring it to a boil and simmer for 5 minutes, stirring occasionally.

Turn off the pot and return the shrimps to the pot. Stir once and transfer to a serving dish.

Sprinkle with spring onions and serve immediately.

Salmon with Apricot Salsa

Servings: 4

Ingredients:

For cooking:

- 1 tsp avocado oil

For salmon:

- 1 lb salmon fillets, cut into 4 equal pieces

- 1 small onion, finely chopped

- 1 garlic clove, minced

- 1 tsp sea salt

- ¼ tsp red pepper chili flakes

- ¼ tsp cayenne pepper, ground

For apricot salsa:

- 2 large apricots, pitted
- ½ tsp sea salt
- 1 tbsp fresh parsley, finely chopped
- ½ tsp black pepper, ground
- ¼ tsp dried rosemary, ground

Directions:

First, prepare the apricot salsa: simply combine all salsa ingredients in a food processor and blend until smooth. Set aside.

Plug in the Instant Pot and grease the stainless steel insert with some avocado oil. Add onions, garlic, red chili pepper flakes, and cayenne pepper. Stir-fry for 2 minutes and add salmon fillets. Cook for 2 minutes on each side and remove from the pot.

Pour the salsa into the pot and add 2-3 tbsp of water. Close the lid and adjust the steam release handle by moving the valve to the Sealing position. Cook for 2 minutes over Manual mode on High pressure.

When done, perform a quick pressure release and open the pot.

Drizzle the salsa over salmon fillets and serve immediately. Enjoy!

Baked Salmon Foil Packets With Vegetables

Servings: 4

Ingredients

- lbs Salmon (cut into 4 6-oz fillets)
- 1/2 lb Asparagus (trimmed, then cut in half)
- 1/2 tsp Sea salt
- 1 tbsp Fresh dill (chopped)
- 1/4 cup Olive oil
- 2 cloves Garlic (minced)
- 10 oz Grape tomatoes
- 1/4 tsp Black pepper

- 1/2 medium lemon (juiced and zested; about 1 tbsp juice and ½ tbsp zest)

- 10 oz Zucchini (sliced into half moons)

- 1 tbsp Fresh parsley (chopped)

Directions

1. Preheat the oven to 400oF or preheat the grill to medium.

2. Layout 4 large squares of foil [at least 12x12 inches (30x30 cm)]. Put a salmon fillet in the center of each piece of foil. Divide the veggies squarely among the foil around the salmon.

3. In a small bowl, whisk together the olive oil, black pepper, parsley, sea salt, lemon juice, minced garlic, lemon zest, and dill.

4. Use about half of the oil mixture to skirmish the salmon, getting most of the garlic onto the salmon.

Pour the residual oil mixture evenly over the veggies. Lightly sprinkle more salt and pepper over the salmon and veggies.

5. Fold the foil over and seal shut to form packets.

Place onto a baking sheet.

6. Bake for about 15-20 minutes, or grill (enclosed) for 13-18 minutes, until the salmon flakes easily with a fork or is done to your liking.

Garlic Shrimps with Broccoli

Servings: 4

Ingredients:

For cooking:

- 1 cup fish stock

- 1 tsp coconut oil

For garlic shrimps:

- 1 lb shrimps, peeled and deveined

- 4 garlic cloves, finely chopped

- 1 tsp fresh ginger, grated

- 1 tsp cornstarch

- 2 tbsp soy sauce, low-sodium

- 1 medium-sized red onion, finely chopped

- ½ tsp salt

For broccoli:

- 1 cup broccoli, chopped into florets

- ½ tsp Italian seasoning

- ¼ tsp red pepper flakes

Directions:

Plug in the Instant Pot and pour the fish stock in the stainless steel insert. Add broccoli and sprinkle with Italian seasoning and red pepper flakes. Securely lock the lid and set the steam release handle. Cook for 2 minutes using the Manual mode on High pressure.

When done, perform a quick pressure release and open the pot. Drain the broccoli and transfer to a bowl. Cover with a lid and set aside. Reserve the fish stock.

Now, add shrimps and close the lid again. Set the steam release handle and press the Manual button. Set the timer for 1 minute and cook on High pressure.

When done, open the pot and press the Sauté button. Add garlic, onions, and ginger. Stir-fry for 1 minute and then stir in the cornstarch and soy sauce. Continue to cook for another 2-3 minutes or until the sauce thickens. Sprinkle with some salt and give it a good stir. Turn off the pot.

Serve creamy shrimps with broccoli and enjoy!

Slow Cooker Tacos

Servings: 2

Ingredients:

- 6 inch tortillas (8)

- Bay leaves (2)

- Ground black pepper (to taste)

- Thyme (.25 tsp. dried)

- Cilantro (1 cup chopped)

- Cayenne pepper (.25 tsp.)

- Cinnamon (.5 tsp.)

- Cumin (.5 tsp. ground)

- Chuck roast (2 lbs. beef, cubed)

- Garlic (8 cloves minced)

- Onion (1 chopped)

- Tomatoes (2 chopped)

- 2 jalapeno peppers (chopped, seeded)

- Oil (1 T)

DIRECTIONS

Add the oil to a skillet and place it on the stove over a burner set to a medium/high heat.

Add in the garlic as well as the onion, tomatoes and peppers and let them cook for 5 minutes before removing them from the pan and adding them to a blender with 1 tsp. salt and .5 cups water and blend well.

Add the results back into the skillet before mixing in the beef and turning the burner to medium and let it brown.

Mix in the cayenne pepper, cinnamon and cumin and let everything cook for an additional minute.

As this cooks, add 1.5 cups of water as well as the thyme and cilantro into the blender and blend well.

Add all of the ingredients to the slow cooker and let them cook, covered, on a low heat for 6 hours.

Discard the bay leaves prior to adding the ingredients to the tortillas and serving.

Fish Amandine

Servings: 4

Ingredients

- 4 ounce fresh or frozen skinless tilapia, trout or halibut fillets, 1/2- to 1-inch thick

- ¼ cup buttermilk

- ½ teaspoon dry mustard

- ⅛ teaspoon crushed red pepper

- 1 tablespoon butter, melted

- ¼ teaspoon salt

- ½ cup panko bread crumbs or fine dry bread crumbs

- 2 tablespoons chopped fresh parsley or 2 teaspoons dried parsley flakes

- ¼ cup sliced almonds, coarsely chopped

- 2 tablespoons grated Parmesan cheese

Directions

1. Defrost fish, if frozen. Preheat oven to 450oF.

Grease a shallow baking pan; set aside. Rinse fish; pat dry with paper towels.

2. Pour buttermilk into a shallow dish. In an extra shallow dish, mix bread crumbs, dry mustard, parsley, and salt. Dip fish into buttermilk, then into crumb mixture, turning to coat. Place coated fish in the ready baking pan.

3. Sprinkle fish with almonds and Parmesan cheese; drizzle with melted butter. Sprinkle with crinkled red pepper. Bake for 5 minutes per 1/2-inch thickness of fish or until fish flakes easily when checked with a fork.

Sweet Apple Trout

Servings: 4

Ingredients:

For cooking:

- 1 tsp sesame oil

For shrimp scampi:

- 7 oz trout fillets, cut into bite-sized pieces

- 1 medium-sized Granny Smiths apple, cut into bite-sized pieces

- 1 tsp soy sauce

- 1 tsp rice vinegar

- 1 tsp lemon juice, freshly squeezed

Seasoning:

- ½ tsp sea salt

- 1 tbsp fresh parsley, finely chopped

- ½ tsp black pepper, ground

- ¼ tsp dried rosemary, ground

Directions:

In a large bowl, combine soy sauce, rice vinegar, lemon juice, sea salt, parsley, black pepper, and rosemary. Mix until combined and brush the fish with this mixture.

Plug in the Instant Pot and grease the stainless steel insert with sesame oil. Press the Sauté button and add fish and apple. Cook for 2 minutes, stirring occasionally.

Add enough water to cover and securely lock the lid. Adjust the steam release handle and press the Manual button. Set the timer for 2 minutes and cook on High pressure.

When you hear the cookers end signal, perform a quick pressure release by turning the valve to the Venting position. Open the pot and transfer to a serving plate. Enjoy!

Side Dish Recipes

Chicken Liver with Herbs

Servings: 4

Ingredients

- 600 g chicken liver
- 1 minced onion
- 1 minced garlic clove
- 1/2 packet parsley
- 1/2 packet cilantro
- Pepper and salt, to taste
- Bundle of herbs (thyme and bay leaf)
- 1 tbsp. sunflower oil
- 1 cube 0% fat chicken broth

Direction

Mix and let chicken liver marinate with chopped onions and garlic, a pinch of pepper, salt, and a bundle of herbs for 10 minutes.

Dilute the chicken stock cube in 500ml of hot water.

Sauté the mixture with a tablespoon of sunflower oil and add the diluted chicken broth.

Cook in air fryer for 30 minutes.

Add coriander and parsley to the end. Serve and enjoy!

Kani and Shrimp Fry with Champignon

Servings: 4

Ingredients

- 2 garlic cloves
- 1 packet parsley

- 500 g mushrooms
- 500 g Kani
- 500 g prawns

Direction

Chop the garlic and parsley at the same time and set aside.

Wash the mushrooms, drain and chop them. Reserve.

Cut the Kani sticks into cubes.

Peel the prawns and cut into cubes.

In a nonstick air fryer, sauté the shrimps in the air fryer and then the mushrooms.

Let the water evaporate for one minute.

Then add the Kanis. Season and add garlic and parsley mixture and serve immediately. Enjoy!

Smoked Chicken Patties

Servings: 2

Ingredients

- 7 egg whites
- 60 ml water
- 1 tbsp. cornstarch
- 175 g smoked chicken breast
- 200 g minced mushrooms
- 2 minced onions
- 2 tbsp. 0% fat cottage cheese
- 1 tbsp. chopped chives
- 20 boiled chives stalks in water, to make them flexible
- Black pepper and salt, to taste

Direction

Mix egg whites, water, and cornstarch.

Heat a nonstick air fryer in air fryer and cook the spoon-to-spoon mixture to get 20 round pies 10cm in diameter.

Wipe off excess water with a paper towel and let cool room temperature.

In medium heat in the air fryer, sauté the chopped chicken, mushrooms, and chopped onions in a lightly oiled frying pan.

Lower the heat and add the cottage cheese, sprinkle with the chives and sprinkle black pepper and salt as per your taste.

Divide the stuffing between the 20 pies and close in a pie shape with the help of the chive stalks.

Store in a cool place and serve at room temperature. Enjoy!

Crispy Chicken Wings

Servings: 2

Ingredients

- 3 pairs chicken wings
- 1 small cup light soy sauce
- 1 garlic clove, mashed
- 1 tbsp. liquid sweetener
- 4 tsp. condiments (cloves, peppers, cinnamon, fennel and star anise)
- 1 tsp. chopped fresh ginger

Direction

Mix all ingredients in a container.

Marinate for two to three hours, stirring occasionally.

Place in the air fryer in a pan to bake and cook.

When the chicken wings begin to brown (in 5-10 minutes).

Turn them over and let them cook for another 5-10 minutes. Serve and enjoy!

Vegetable Pudding

Servings: 2

Ingredients

- 4 eggs
- 1 pinch nutmeg
- 500 ml skimmed milk
- 1 tbsp. finely chopped herbs
- 200 g chopped vegetables (tomato, zucchini, broccoli, eggplant, carrot)
- Black pepper and salt, to taste

Direction

Beat egg with the spices and add the warm milk.

Add the vegetables and cook in 180 degree air fryer for 15 minutes. Serve and enjoy!

Fish in the Paper

Servings: 4

Ingredients

- 2 onions
- 2 tomatoes
- 2 carrots
- 1 green bell pepper
- 2 sprigs celery
- 2 sprigs parsley
- 4 slices lean fish
- Black pepper and salt

Direction

Preheat air fryer to 250 degrees.

Chop the onions, tomatoes, carrots, peppers, celery, and parsley.

Season adequately using salt along with pepper.

Wash and dry the fish. On a sheet of parchment paper, place the fish and chopped vegetables.

Close the papers tightly and cook at 180 degrees. Serve and enjoy!

Rolls of Smoked Salmon

Servings: 3

Ingredients

- 3 eggs
- 3 tbsp. water
- 3 tbsp. cornstarch
- 250 g 0% fat cottage cheese
- 2 tbsp. minced chives
- 1 tbsp. minced ginger
- 100 g smoked salmon
- Some parsley leaves
- Black pepper, to taste

Direction

Mix an egg, a tablespoon of water, a teaspoon of cornstarch and make a thin omelet in an air fryer.

Repeat the operation with the rest of the eggs, water, and cornstarch.

Spread cottage cheese gently on each omelet, sprinkle with chives, and ginger.

Distribute the salmon and add black pepper. Roll up the omelets, squeezing tightly on a movie paper.

Store in the freezer for three hours.

Cut into slices with a sharp knife and serve on a plate decorated with parsley. Enjoy!

Stuffed Chicken Breast

Servings: 5

Ingredients

- 10 thinly slice chicken breast fillets
- 3 tbsp. soy light
- 350 ml Coke Zero
- 1 onion
- Freshly grated ginger
- Garlic
- Salt, to taste
- 1 packet spinach
- 300 g light ricotta
- 2 tbsp. 0% fat creamy curd

Direction

Let chicken fillets marinate in light soy sauce and Coke for about 2 hours.

Sauté spinach, add ricotta and curd.

Fill the fillets with the spinach cream, roll up, and secure the ends with sticks.

Put in an air fryer proof dish, cook with soy sauce.

Cover with aluminum foil so as not to dry and cook for about 15 minutes.

Remove the aluminum foil and leave gild.

Serve with creamy spinach cream. Enjoy!

Marinated Chicken Skewers

Servings: 4

Ingredients

- 4 chicken breasts
- 4 garlic cloves
- 2 lemons

- 1 tsp. cumin powder

- 1 tsp. thyme

- 1 green or red bell pepper

- 8 onions

- Salt and pepper, to taste

Direction

The day before, cut the chicken breasts into pieces, place them on a deep plate with the minced garlic, lemon juice, cumin, thyme, black pepper along with salt.

Cover with film paper and marinate in the refrigerator until the next day.

Dice the bell pepper and peeled onions, then prepare the skewers, interspersing the chicken and vegetables.

Brush the sauce and cook on the air fryer grill for 5 minutes each side. Serve and enjoy!

Eggplant Pudding

Servings: 2

Ingredients

- 400 g eggplant

- 3 eggs

- 200 ml skimmed milk

- Nutmeg

- Some thyme stems

- Some rosemary stems

- Black pepper and salt

Direction

Wash and peel the eggplants, cut into slices and set aside in a colander.

Let it pour for 30 minutes by adding a little salt.

Dry the slices before cooking in boiling water for 5 minutes and then drain again.

Preheat air fryer to 150 degrees.

Make an omelet and season.

Mix in milk and scrape off some of the nutmeg. Sprinkle thyme and rosemary.

In a baking form, arrange eggplant slices and pour egg mixture with milk on top.

Cook for 30 minutes. Serve and enjoy!

Chicken Heart Skewers with Herbs

Servings: 4

Ingredients

- 500 g chicken heart
- 1 minced onion
- 1 minced garlic clove
- Salt and pepper, to taste
- Herbs (rosemary, fennel, basil, thyme and lavender)
- 1 red bell pepper
- 1 green bell pepper
- 16 wooden skewers

Direction

Marinate Chicken heart in garlic, herbs, salt along with pepper for 10 minutes.

Cut the onion and bell pepper into large squares.

Make skewers of chicken hearts with peppers and onions (1 chicken heart, 1 onion, 1 bell pepper (red), 1 bell pepper (green). Repeat 3 times).

Cook in air fryer for 10 minutes. Serve and enjoy!

Chicken Curry and Yogurt Escallops

Servings: 4

Ingredients

- 25 g nonfat natural yogurt
- 3 tbsp. curry
- 4 chicken escallops

- Black pepper and salt, to taste

Direction

Prepare the barbecue embers.

Mix together yogurts, Black pepper and salt, and curry powder.

Marinate the escallops for 2 hours in the refrigerator.

Grill the escallops for 5 minutes in an air fryer by dipping them once or twice in the marinade during cooking. Serve and enjoy!

Dessert and soup Recipes

Date Sweetened Instant Pot Carrot Cake

Servings: 8

Ingredients:

Dry Ingredients:

- 3/4 teaspoon of baking soda

- 1/4 teaspoon of ground cardamom

- 1/4 teaspoon of salt

- 3/4 teaspoon of baking powder

- 1/2 teaspoon of ground cinnamon

- 1/4 teaspoon of Ground Ginger

- 1 +1/2 cup of whole wheat pastry flour

- 1/4 teaspoon of ground allspice

Wet Ingredients:

- 1/4 cup of avocado

- 1/2 cup of non-dairy milk

- 1/2 teaspoon of orange flower water

- Two tablespoons of ground flaxseeds mixed with 1/4 cup warm water

- Cake Mix In Ingredients:

- One cup of dates (chopped)

- One cup of carrot (shredded)

Icing Ingredients:

- 1/2 cup of water

- 1/2 cup of cashews

- 1 +1/2 teaspoons of orange flavor water

- 1/2 cup of dates (chopped)

Directions

Take a large mixing bowl and whisk all the dry ingredients in it.

Take another mixing bowl and add all the wet ingredients and mix in ingredients in it, mix thoroughly until well combined.

Now mix the dry and wet mixture, give it a good stir.

Take a cake pan that fits inside your instant pot and grease it well and pour the cake batter in it.

Switch on your multi-pressure cooker, such as instant pot, and pour one cup of water in it.

Set the steamer rack or trivet inside the pot and carefully lower the cake pan on the rack.

Lock the instant pot and bake the cake on the manual or high-pressure method for 50 minutes, allow the pressure to release naturally.

Now make the icing for the cake by adding cashews water and dates in a saucepan and boil it.

Allow the mixture to cool at room temperature.

Once the mixture is cooled enough, add it into the food processor and blend until a smooth paste is formed.

Open the instant pot and insert a toothpick in the bread to see if the cake is baked properly, carefully take the cake pan out of the pot and let it cool at room temperature for 10 minutes.

Ice the cake and chill it in the refrigerator.

Enjoy.

Instant Pot Tapioca Pudding

Servings: 8

Ingredients:

- 14 ounces of coconut milk
- 2 cups of mango puree (unsweetened)
- 1/2 teaspoon of vanilla extra
- 1/3 cup of tapioca pearls (rinsed)

- 1 cup of mango (cut into small chunks)

- 1/2 cup of water

- Two ripe bananas

For Garnishing:

- Mango Cubes

Directions

Do not use the tapioca pearls that are used to make bubbly tea, Wash and rinse the topica pearls well and set the pearls aside for 15 minutes.

Mash the mango pure and banana to make a smooth paste.

Take a safe oven bowl that fits inside your instant pot and add the mashed paste along with other remaining ingredients into the bowl, mix well.

Take out your multi-pressure cooker, such as instant pot, and pour water in it.

Set the steamer rack or trivet inside the instant pot and carefully lower the bowl on the steamer rack.

Lock the instant pot and cook the tapioca pudding on the manual or high-pressure method for 10 minutes, allow the pressure to release quickly.

Open the instant pot and carefully take out the pudding bowl and cover it with Aluminium foil, allowed to cool at room temperature.

Garnish the pudding with mango cubes and refrigerate your delicious tapioca pudding before serving.

Instant Pot Banana Bread

Servings: 4

Ingredients:

Dry Ingredients:

- 1/4 teaspoon of baking soda

- 3/4 cups of all-purpose flour

- A pinch of salt

- 1/2 teaspoons of baking powder

Wet Ingredients:

- 1/4 cup of milk

- 1/2 teaspoon of vanilla extract

- Three tablespoons of oil

- 1/2 cup of mashed banana

- 1/4 cup of sugar

Toppings:

- Slivered Almonds

- Hershey Chocolate Syrup

Directions

Take a mixing bowl and whisk all the dry ingredients in it, set the bowl aside.

Take another mixing bowl and put sugar, banana, oil, and vanilla extract in it, mix thoroughly.

Add the dry ingredients in the mashed banana mixture, mix well to combine, but do not over mix.

Take a bundt pan that fits inside your instant pot and grease it with oil, then dust the pan with flour.

Pour the banana batter into the pan and cover it tightly with aluminum foil.

Switch on your multi-pressure cooker, such as instant pot, and pour one cup of water in it.

Set the steamer rack or trivet inside the pot and carefully lower the cake pan on the rack.

Lock the instant pot and bake the banana bread on the manual or high pressure method for 35 minutes, allow the pressure to release naturally.

Open the instant pot and insert a toothpick in the bread to see if the bread is cooked properly, take the cake pan out of the pot and let it cool at room temperature for 10 minutes.

Carefully take the bread out in a plate, top it with chocolate sauce and almonds, enjoy.

Instant Pot Middle Eastern Lamb Stew

Servings: 4

Ingredients:

- Two tablespoons of ghee
- One onion (chopped)
- 1 + 3 / 4 pounds of lamb shoulder meat (cut into one and half inch cube)
- Six garlic cloves (grated)
- One teaspoon of cumin powder
- One teaspoon of cinnamon
- One teaspoon of coriander powder
- Salt and pepper, as you like
- One teaspoon of turmeric powder
- Two tablespoons of tomato paste
- 1/2 teaspoon of chili flakes
- 1/4 cup of apple cider vinegar
- Two tablespoons of tomato paste
- 1 + 1/4 cups of chicken broth
- Two tablespoons of brown sugar
- 15 ounces of canned chickpeas (washed and drained)
- 1/4 cup of raisins (chopped)

Directions

Turn on your multi pressure cooker, such as instant pot and select the saute mode.

Add oil into the pot and let it heat; once the oil is heated enough, stir fry onions in it for 3 minutes, until translucent and soft.

Then add garlic and all the spices and seasonings and stir fry for five more minutes, until fragrant.

Then add tomato paste, vinegar, broth, honey, raisins and chickpeas and mix all the ingredients well.

Lock the instant pot and prepare the stew on high pressure or manual mode for 50 minutes, allowing the pressure to release naturally.

Open the instant pot, taste and adjust the seasonings and give the stew a good stir.

Your delicious and easy lamb stew is ready to serve, enjoy hot.

Instant Pot Baked Apples

Servings: 4

Ingredients:

- Four small Gala apples (1/4 pound each)
- One teaspoon of cinnamon
- One teaspoon of brown sugar
- One teaspoon of coconut oil
- Four tablespoons of walnuts (chopped)
- Eight frozen cranberries

Directions

Cut the center of the apples to make room for filling, but do not cut from the bottom.

Take a mixing bowl and whisk walnuts, cinnamon, and brown sugar together.

Fill the apples with a walnut filling and divide two cranberries for each apple.

Top each apple with 1/4 teaspoon of coconut oil.

Switch on your multi-pressure cooker, such as instant pot, and pour one cup of water in it.

Set the steamer rack or trivet inside the pot and carefully put the apples on the rack.

Lock the instant pot and bake the apples on manual or pressure cooker method for 3 minutes, allow the pressure to release quickly.

Unlock the instant pot and carefully take out the baked apple.

Enjoy.

Instant Pot Moroccan Stew

Servings: 6

Ingredients:

- Two tablespoons of olive oil
- Four cups of butternut squash (cubed)
- One cup of onion (chopped)
- One tablespoon of ginger (grated)
- 1 cup of carrots (cut into 1 inch thick pieces)
- One tablespoon of garlic (grated)
- One teaspoon of cumin of powder
- One teaspoon of turmeric powder
- One teaspoon of coriander powder
- 1/2 teaspoon of cayenne pepper
- 14.5 ounces of canned tomatoes (diced)
- One preserved lemon (chopped)
- 2 cups of vegetable broth
- A Pinch of saffron
- 2 cups of cooked chickpeas
- Heavy cream
- Salt and pepper, as you like
- For Garnishing:
- Chopped Cilantro

Directions

Turn on your multi pressure cooker, such as instant pot and select the saute mode.

Add oil into the pot and let it heat; once the oil is heated enough, stir fry onions in it for 1 minute until translucent and soft.

Then add ginger and garlic and stir fry for 30 seconds.

Now add all the seasonings and spices into the sauteed vegetables and stir fry by stirring continuously, until fragrant.

Switch off the saute mode and pour four tablespoons of vegetable broth to deglaze the pot, then pour the remaining vegetable broth, carrots, preserved lemon and butternut squash cubes, stir well to combine.

Now add tomatoes and push it down with the help of a spatula, do not stir the tomatoes.

Lock the instant pot and prepare the stew on high pressure or manual mode for 6 minutes, allowing the pressure to release quickly.

Open the instant pot, taste and adjust the seasonings and switch on the saute mode again.

Add saffron, heavy cream and chickpeas give the stew a good stir.

Your delicious vegetable stew is ready to serve, garnish it with cilantro and enjoy hot.

Instant Pot Smoky Lentil and Potato Soup

Servings: 6

Ingredients:

- 1/2 cup of onions (diced)

- One tablespoon of olive oil

- 1/2 cup of carrots (chopped)

- Three garlic cloves (minced)

- Two stalks of celery (diced)

- 1 + 1/2 teaspoons of smoked paprika

- Two teaspoons of ground cumin

- One pound of red potatoes (cut into 1 inch cubes)

- 1 cup of brown lentils (washed and drained)

- 1 cup of red lentils (rinsed and drained)

- 8 cups of vegetable broth or chicken broth

- 10 ounces of spinach (chopped)

- Salt, as you like

Directions

Switch on your multi pressure cooker, such as instant pot and select the saute function.

Add oil into the pot and let it heat; once the oil is heated enough stir fry onions, carrots, garlic and celery in it for 2 minutes until soft. Stir continuously.

Then add paprika, salt and cumin into the pot and stir fry for one more minute.

Turn off the saute mode and add lentils, potatoes and broth, mix well to combine.

Lock the instant pot and prepare the soup on manual or pressure cooker method for 3 minutes let the steam to release on natural mode.

The soup is cooked, open the instant pot and stir in the spinach and let it wilt, taste and adjust the salt and pepper, serve hot and enjoy.

Instant Pot Vegetable Stew

Servings: 8

Ingredients:

- One tablespoon of olive oil

- One celery stalk (chopped)

- Two tablespoons of corn starch

- 1/2 onion (chopped)

- 4 ounces of frozen peas

- Two garlic cloves (grated)

- Two medium Yukon gold potatoes (chopped)

- Two carrots (chopped)

- 2 cup of green beans (chopped)

- 8 ounces of white button mushrooms

- 1/4 cup of low sodium vegetable broth

- 8 ounces of Portobello mushrooms (chopped)

- One teaspoon of Rosemary

- One teaspoon of Italian seasoning

- 1/2 teaspoon of rubbed sage

- 15 ounces of canned tomatoes (diced)

- 1/2 cup of red wine

- 1/2 teaspoon of kitchen bouquet

- One tablespoon of balsamic vinegar

- Salt and pepper, as you like

Directions

Turn on your multi pressure cooker, such as instant pot and select the saute mode.

Add oil into the pot and let it heat; once the oil is heated enough, stir fry celery, onions, garlic, and carrots in it, until translucent and soft.

Then add rosemary, Italian seasoning and sage and stir well to combine.

Put mushrooms into the sauteed vegetables and stir fry to evaporate all the liquid from the instant pot.

Switch off the saute mode and pour wine to deglaze the pot, then add tomato sauce, vegetable broth, and tomatoes, stir well to combine.

Now put all the remaining vegetables (except for pearl onions and peas) and seasonings mix all the stew ingredients to combine well.

Lock the instant pot and prepare the stew on high pressure or manual mode for 15 minutes, allowing the pressure to release naturally.

To make the corn starch slurry, mix it with water and make sure the paste is lump free.

Open the instant pot, taste and adjust the seasonings and add slurry, peas and pearl onions, give the stew a good stir.

Your delicious vegetable stew is ready to serve, enjoy hot.

Instant Pot Ethiopian Lentil Stew

Servings: 3

Ingredients:

- 1 inch Ginger piece (grated)
- One onion (thinly sliced)
- Two tablespoons of tomato paste
- Two garlic cloves (grated)
- Three green onion stalks (diced)
- 1.5 tablespoon of olive oil
- Two teaspoons of berbere Spice
- 1/2 teaspoons of cumin powder
- 3/4 cup of red lentils
- 25 baby spinach leaves
- 2 cups of vegetable broth
- Salt and pepper, as you like

For Garnishing:

- Chopped Cilantro

Directions

Turn on your multi pressure cooker, such as instant pot and select the saute mode.

Add oil into the pot and let it heat; once the oil is heated enough stir fry garlic, onions, ginger and spring onions for 3 minutes, until soft.

Then add all the spices in the sauteed vegetables and stir fry until fragrant.

Now put lentils and tomato paste and stir fry for 30 seconds.

Switch off the saute mode and pour 1.5 cups of vegetable broth into the instant pot.

Lock the instant pot and prepare the stew on high pressure or manual mode for 6 minutes, allowing the pressure to release quickly.

Open the instant pot, taste and adjust the seasonings and put the remaining vegetable broth and spinach leaves, give the stew a good stir and let the spinach wilt.

Your delicious stew is ready to serve, enjoy hot.

Instant Pot Caramel Sauce

Servings: 2

Ingredients:

- 3/4 cup of pure maple syrup

- One teaspoon of pure vanilla extract

- 1 (14-ounces) of canned coconut cream

- 1/4 cup of coconut oil

- A pinch of sea salt

Directions

Switch on your multi-pressure cooker, such as instant pot, and turn on the saute mode.

Stir in maple syrup, oil, and coconut cream in it.

Let the cream sauce boil for 15 minutes, stir the sauce frequently.

Turn off the instant pot and mix vanilla extract and salt in the sauce, let it cool at room temperature for a few minutes, enjoy.

You can store the left sauce in an airtight container.

Instant Pot Vegan Thai Coconut Rice Pudding

Servings: 8

Ingredients:

- 4 + 1/2 cups of unsweetened coconut milk beverage(divided)

- Two tablespoons of maple syrup

- 1/2 teaspoon of ground turmeric

- 1 + 1/2 teaspoon of vanilla extract

- 1+ 1/2 cup of golden raisins

- 2 cups of Jasmine rice (dried)
- Two tablespoons of coconut cream
- 1/2 teaspoon of ground ginger
- 1/2 teaspoon of coconut extract

Directions

Take out your multi-pressure cooker, such as instant pot and rice and coconut milk in it.

Lock the instant pot and prepare the pudding on the manual or high-pressure method for 3 minutes, letting the pressure to release naturally for 10 minutes.

Then quickly release the remaining pressure.

Open the instant pot and mix the remaining ingredients in it, give it a good stir.

Garnish with more gold raisins, refrigerate it before serving and enjoy.

Instant Pot Vegan Apple Crumble

Servings: 4

Ingredients:

- 1/4 cup of Spelt flour
- 1/2 teaspoon of salt
- Five medium honey crisp apple (peeled and cut into small cubes)
- 1/2 cup of water
- 3/4 cup of quick oats
- 1/4 cup of coconut sugar
- 1/4 cup of coconut oil
- Two teaspoons of cinnamon
- One tablespoon of maple syrup

Directions

Take a mixing bowl and whisk oats, sugar, flour, and salt in melted coconut oil, stir well to combine

Then coat the oats into the mixture and set the bowl aside.

Switch on your multi-pressure cooker, such as instant pot, and add apples into the pot and sprinkle cinnamon over them.

Then pour maple syrup over the apples and add water into the instant pot.

Lock the instant pot and cook apples on the manual or high-pressure method for 8 minutes, allow the pressure to release naturally.

Your sweet crumbled apples are ready to serve, enjoy with vegan ice cream.

Instant Pot Vegan Thai Coconut Rice Pudding

Servings: 8

Ingredients:

- 4 + 1/2 cups of unsweetened coconut milk beverage (divided)
- Two tablespoons of maple syrup
- 1/2 teaspoon of ground turmeric
- 1 + 1/2 teaspoon of vanilla extract
- 1+ 1/2 cup of golden raisins
- 2 cups of Jasmine rice (dried)
- Two tablespoons of coconut cream
- 1/2 teaspoon of ground ginger
- 1/2 teaspoon of coconut extract

Directions

Take out your multi-pressure cooker, such as instant pot and rice and coconut milk in it.

Lock the instant pot and prepare the pudding on the manual or high pressure method for 3 minutes, letting the pressure to release naturally for 10 minutes.

Then quickly release the remaining pressure.

Open the instant pot and mix the remaining ingredients in it, give it a good stir.

Garnish with more gold raisins, chill the pudding in the fridge before serving and enjoy.

Instant Pot Red Lentil Soup

Servings: 8

Ingredients:

- 1 cup of onion (chopped)
- Two tablespoons of olive oil
- 5 cups of celery (chopped)
- One cup of carrots (chopped)
- Two cans (14.5 ounces) of fire roasted tomatoes
- 2 cups of water
- 1 cup of low sodium vegetable broth
- One teaspoon of ground cumin
- 1.5 cup of split red lentils (washed and drained)
- Salt and pepper, as you like
- 1/2 teaspoon of thyme (dried)
- One tablespoon of red wine vinegar
- 2 cups of fresh baby spinach (chopped)
- Heavy cream

Directions

Switch on your multi pressure cooker, such as instant pot and select the saute function.

Add oil into the pot and let it heat; once the oil is heated enough stir fry onions, celery and carrots in it for 5 minutes until the vegetables are tender.

Then add garlic into the pot and stir fry for one more minute.

Turn off the saute mode and add vegetable broth, tomatoes, lentils, water, and seasonings into the instant pot and stir well to combine.

Lock the instant pot and prepare the soup on manual or pressure cooker method for 10 minutes let the steam to release on natural mode for 10 minutes.

Then quickly release the remaining steam.

The soup is cooked, open the instant pot, and take out 2 cups of soup, then puree the remaining soup with the help of an immersion blender, and stir in the vinegar, spinach and 2 cups of not blended soup.

Turn on the saute mode again and cook the soup to wilt the spinach.

Your soup is ready to serve, taste and adjust the salt and pepper, top it with heavy cream and enjoy.

Instant Pot Mango Cake with Cardamom

Servings: 4

Ingredients:

- 1/4 cup of almond oil

- 3/4 cup of all-purpose flour

- 1/4 cup of vegan yogurt

- 1/4 teaspoon of baking soda

- 1/4 teaspoon of turmeric powder

- 1/3 cup of mango puree

- 1/4 cup of powdered sugar

- 1/8 teaspoon of salt

- 0.625 teaspoon of baking powder

- 1/4 teaspoon of cardamom powder

Directions

Take a large mixing bowl and whisk sugar and yogurt in it, until the sugar is dissolved.

Then stir in baking soda, salt, and baking powder and keep the bowl aside for 5 minutes.

When the mixture is emulsified, add in the oil, cardamom powder, turmeric powder, and mango puree, stir well.

Now add flour into the cake batter and mix until well combined, make sure the cake batter is lump-free.

Take a cake pan that fits inside your instant pot and grease it well and pour the cake batter in it and cover the pan with Aluminium foil.

Switch on your multi-pressure cooker, such as instant pot, and pour one and a half cup of water in it.

Set the steamer rack or trivet inside the pot and carefully lower the cake pan on the rack.

Lock the instant pot and bake the mango cake on low pressure or cake mode for 25 minutes, allow the pressure to release naturally.

Open the instant pot and insert a toothpick in the bread to see if the cake is baked properly, carefully take the cake pan out of the pot and let it cool at room temperature.

Cut the cake into slices and serve with fresh fruits, enjoy.

Instant Pot Red Beans and Rice Stew

Servings: 8

Ingredients:

- One onion (diced)
- One tablespoon of olive oil
- One green bell pepper (diced)
- Four garlic cloves (grated)
- 1/2 cup of celery (chopped)
- Two cans of 15 ounces of red kidney beans (drained and rinsed)
- 15 ounces of canned diced tomatoes (no sugar and low salt)
- One tablespoon of smoked paprika
- 1/2 teaspoon of liquid smoke
- Two teaspoons of oregano (dried)
- One tablespoon of thyme (dried)
- 3/4 cup of brown rice (uncooked)
- 1/2 teaspoon of Cayenne pepper
- Salt and pepper, as you like

Directions

Turn on your multi pressure cooker, such as instant pot and select the saute mode.

Add oil into the pot and let it heat; once the oil is heated enough stir fry garlic, bell peppers, celery, and onions for 5 minutes, until soft.

Switch off the saute mode and add remaining ingredients into the instant pot, stir well to combine.

Lock the instant pot and prepare the stew on high pressure or manual mode for 15 minutes, allowing the pressure to release naturally.

Open the instant pot, taste and adjust the seasonings and give the stew a good stir.

Your delicious and easy beans and rice stew.

Instant Pot Mung Bean Stew

Servings: 3

Ingredients:

- Two garlic cloves (grated)
- One tablespoon of coconut oil
- 1 lb ground pork (minced)
- 1/2 onion (chopped)
- 3 cups of water
- 1 cup of mung beans (washed and rinsed)
- 2 cups of spinach
- Salt, as you like

Directions

Turn on your multi pressure cooker, such as instant pot and select the saute mode.

Add oil into the pot and let it heat; once the oil is heated enough and stir fry onions and garlic in it for 3 minutes.

Then add minced pork into the sauteed vegetables and stir fry until light brown.

Switch off the saute mode and mix remaining ingredients (except for spinach) into the sauteed vegetables.

Lock the instant pot and prepare the stew on manual or high-pressure method for 10 minutes, allowing the pressure to release naturally.

Open the instant pot, taste and adjust the salt, stir in the spinach and let it wilt.

Serve hot and enjoy.

Instant Pot Taiwanese Beef Noodle Soup

Servings: 10

Ingredients:

- Two tablespoons of olive oil
- 3 pounds of beef Shank (cut into 2 inch cubes)
- Six garlic cloves (grated)
- 2 inch ginger piece (grated)
- One onion (chopped)
- Three scallions (cut into two inch piece)
- Four dried chilies (crushed)
- One tomato (chopped)
- Two tablespoons of spicy bean paste
- One tablespoon of tomato paste
- 1/2 cup of soy sauce
- Two teaspoons of sugar
- 1/2 cup of Shaoxing wine
- 32 ounces of white noodles
- For Spice Sachet:
- 1 Chinese cinnamon stick
- 4 star anise
- One tablespoon of fennel seeds
- Three bay leaves
- One teaspoon of coriander seeds

- One tablespoon of cumin seeds

- 1/4 teaspoon of five spice powder

- Two tablespoons of Sichuan peppercorns

- 1/4 teaspoon of black pepper

- To make a spice sachet wrap all the spice in a small cheese cloth.

For Garnishing:

- Chopped Cilantro

- Chopped Scallions

- A small handful of Bok Choy

- Pickled Mustard Greens

Directions

Take a cooking pot and pour water in it and let it boil on a stovetop. Once the water is boiled, add beef in it and boil it for one minute. Drain the water completely and set the beef aside.

Switch on your multi pressure cooker, such as instant pot and turn on the saute mode.

Add the oil into the pot and let it heat; once the oil is heated enough stir fry ginger, garlic, scallions and onions in it until onions are translucent, keep stirring continuously.

Then add tomatoes and dried chilies in the sauteed vegetables and stir fry for one more minute.

Now put meat, bean paste, tomato paste, soy sauce, wine and sugar, give it a good stir to combine all the ingredients well and turn off the saute mode.

Pour 8 cups of water into the pot along with spice sachet.

Lock the instant pot and prepare the soup on manual or pressure cooker method for 100 minutes, allow the steam to release quickly.

Boil the noodles.

The soup is cooked, open the instant pot, taste salt and pepper and remove the spice sachet.

Your delicious noodle soup is ready to serve, pour it on serving bowl along with boiled noodles and bok choy, serve hot and enjoy.

Instant Pot Chinese Lamb Stew

Servings: 4

Ingredients:

- Three tablespoons of ginger (grated)
- 1.5 pounds of lamb stew meat
- Four stalks of green onion, separate white and green parts
- Eight garlic cloves (minced)
- 48 grams of Shiitake mushrooms
- One small shallot (chopped)
- Eight water chestnuts
- One cup of cold water
- 90 grams of bean curd sheet
- One tablespoon of Shaoxing wine
- Two tablespoons of Chinese fermented bean curd
- One tablespoon of peanut oil
- Two tablespoons of Chinese fermented red bean curd
- One tablespoon of Chu Hou paste
- One tablespoon of dark soy sauce
- One tablespoon of rock sugar
- One tablespoon of regular soy sauce

For Dipping Sauce:

- 1/2 teaspoon of sugar
- Two cubes of Chinese fermented Bean curd
- One tablespoon of hot water
- 1/2 teaspoon of sesame oil

Directions

Turn on your multi pressure cooker, such as instant pot and select the saute mode.

Add oil into the pot and let it heat; once the oil is heated enough stir fry lamb in it, until the lamb is brown from all sides, for better cooking work in batches.

Then add ginger, garlic, the white part of green onions, and shallots and stir fry for 2 minutes, until fragrant.

Then add mushrooms, Chu Hou paste, water chestnuts, fermented bean curd and fermented red bean curd and stir fry for 4 minutes.

Switch off the saute mode and pour wine into the instant pot to deglaze it.

Add curd sheets, rock sugar, both soy sauces, one cup of cold water and make sure the curd sheets are submerged in water.

Lock the instant pot and prepare the stew on high pressure or manual mode for 50 minutes, allowing the pressure to release naturally.

To make the dipping sauce, whisk all the sauce ingredients together in a mixing bowl and set the bowl aside.

Open the instant pot, taste and adjust the seasonings and add green parts of onions in it, give the stew a good stir.

Your delicious stew is ready to serve, enjoy it with dipping sauce.

Instant Pot Vegetable Soup

Servings: 8

Ingredients:

- One teaspoon of olive oil
- Two teaspoons of garlic (grated)
- One onion (chopped)
- Salt and pepper, as you like
- Two teaspoons of Italian seasoning
- 6 cups of chicken broth or vegetable broth (low sodium)
- Three carrots (chopped)
- 1 lb potatoes (chopped)
- 1 + 1/2 cup of fire roasted tomatoes (diced)

- Two celery ribs (sliced)
- 1 cup of fresh green beans (chopped)
- One cup of spinach (chopped)

Directions

Switch on your instant pot and select the saute function.

Add oil into the pot and let it heat; once the oil is heated enough stir fry onions in it, until soft.

Add Italian seasoning, salt, pepper, and garlic into the pot and stir fry for one more minute.

Turn off the saute mode and add chicken or vegetable broth into the instant pot to deglaze it.

Now add the remaining ingredients (except for spinach) and stir well to combine.

Lock the instant pot and prepare the soup on manual or pressure cooker method for 2 minutes, allowing the steam to release naturally.

The soup is cooked, open the instant pot, and add spinach into the soup, let the spinach wilt.

Your delicious vegetable soup is ready to serve, taste and adjust the salt and pepper, enjoy.

Instant Pot Vegetable Noodle Soup

Servings: 4

Ingredients:

- One garlic clove (grated)
- One onion (diced)
- Two teaspoon of olive oil
- One carrot (diced)
- 1/2 cup of sweet corn
- 1/2 small sweet potato (cubed into small pieces)
- One tablespoon of tomato paste
- 1/4 teaspoon of chili powder

- 1/4 teaspoon of garlic powder

- One teaspoon of paprika powder

- A pinch of dried basil

- 5 cups of vegetable or chicken broth

- Four handfuls of spinach

- 100 grams of your favorite uncooked pasta

- Salt and pepper, as you like

For Garnishing:

- Grated Parmesan Cheese

Directions

Switch on your multi pressure cooker, such as instant pot and turn on the saute mode.

Add the oil into the pot and let it heat; once the oil is heated enough stir fry onions, carrots and garlic in it for two minutes, until soft.

Then add tomato paste, sweet potato and spices in the sauteed vegetables and mix well to combine.

Now put pasta, chicken or vegetable broth, and sweet corns give it a good stir and turn off the saute mode.

Lock the instant pot and prepare the soup on manual or pressure cooker method for 4 minutes, allow the steam to release quickly.

The soup is cooked, open the instant pot, taste salt and pepper and mix in the spinach.

Your delicious noodle soup is ready to serve, pour it on serving bowl and sprinkle grated Parmesan cheese, serve hot and enjoy.

Instant Pot Vegan Lemon Cheesecake

Servings: 8

Ingredients:

- 1 + 1/2 tablespoon of almond (roasted)

- Two packets (8 ounces) of vegan cream cheese, cut into small cubes

- 2 ounces of silken tofu

- One tablespoon of lemon juice

- One teaspoon of vanilla extract

- 12 ginger snaps

- 1/2 tablespoon of vegan margarine

- 1/2 cup of granulated sugar

- Zest of one medium lemon

- 1/2 teaspoon of natural lemon extract

- 2 cups of water

Directions

Take out your food processor and blend ginger snap cookies and almonds on high speed to make cookie crumbs, add melted margarine in the cookie mixture and blend until well combined.

Take a cake pan that fits inside your instant pot and grease it well, press down the cookie mixture into the pot.

Now blend cream cheese in sugar, until smooth, then add lemon juice, zest, vanilla essence, and lemon extract in the cream cheese mixture and blend until a smooth paste is formed.

Spread the paste over the cookie crumbs and cover it with Aluminium foil.

Switch on your multi-pressure cooker, such as instant pot, and pour one cup of water in it.

Set the steamer rack or trivet inside the pot and carefully lower the cake pan on the rack.

Lock the instant pot and bake the cake on the slow cooker method and high temperature for 15 minutes, allow the pressure to release naturally.

Open the instant pot and insert a toothpick in the bread to see if the cake is baked properly, carefully take the cake pan out of the pot and let it cool at room temperature for 10 minutes.

Take the cake out on a plate and cut it in slices.

Enjoy.

Instant Pot Butternut Squash Soup

Servings: 6

Ingredients:

- Four garlic cloves (minced)

- 2 cups of vegetable broth

- 1 Granny Smith Apple (diced)

- One carrot (diced)

- One sprig of fresh sage

- One medium butternut squash (diced)

- One onion (diced)

- Salt and pepper as you like

- A pinch of ground cinnamon

- 1/8 teaspoon of cayenne pepper

- 1/2 cup of coconut milk (unsweetened)

For Garnishing:

- Smoked Paprika

Directions

Switch on your multi pressure cooker, such as instant pot and add all the ingredients (except for coconut milk) in it.

Stir well to combine.

Lock the instant pot and prepare the soup on manual or pressure cooker method for 8 minutes, allow the steam to release quickly.

The soup is cooked, open the instant pot, remove sage and mix coconut milk in the soup.

Puree of the soup with the help of an immersion blender, adjust the salt and pepper and garnish with smoked paprika.

Your delicious soup is ready to serve, enjoy.

Instant Pot Holiday Orange Spice Cake

Servings: 7

Ingredients:

Dry Ingredients:

- 1 + 1/2 teaspoon of ground cinnamon

- 1/2 teaspoon of baking soda

- 1/4 teaspoon of ground cloves

- 1 + 1/4 cup of whole wheat pastry flour

- One teaspoon of ground allspice

- 1/2 teaspoon of baking powder

Wet Ingredients:

- 1/3 cup of maple syrup

- Three tablespoons of melted coconut oil

- 1/2 cup of orange juice with pulp

- Two tablespoons of ground flax seeds

Mix-Ins:

- 3/4 cup of dried Cranberries

- Two tablespoons of orange zest

- 1/2 cup of pecans or walnuts (chopped)

Directions

Take a mixing bowl and stir all the dry ingredients in it.

Take another mixing bowl and add all the wet ingredients, whisk until well combined

Now mix the dry ingredients into the wet ingredients, give it a good stir and fold in the mix-ins.

Take a cake pan that fits inside your instant pot and grease it well and pour the cake batter in it and cover the pan with Aluminium foil.

Switch on your multi-pressure cooker, such as instant pot, and pour one and a half cup of water in it.

Set the steamer rack or trivet inside the pot and carefully lower the cake pan on the rack.

Lock the instant pot and bake the cake on the manual or high-pressure method for 35 minutes, allow the pressure to release naturally.

Open the instant pot and insert a toothpick in the bread to see if the cake is baked properly, carefully take the cake pan out of the pot and let it cool at room temperature.

Cut the cake into slices and enjoy.

Conclusion

I hope this book could provide you with plenty of ideas for recipes that won't just flavor good, they shall carry out the body good as well. The next thing is to stop reading already and to begin cooking up slow cooker recipes you will be capable to feel great about eating.

Consider the recipes outlined above as a starter information and build on them as you move, keeping in mind stage requirements as needed and you will be looking and feeling much better than you ever thought feasible earlier than you could ever imagine.

Thank you and good luck!

Lightning Source UK Ltd.
Milton Keynes UK
UKHW051910050321
379874UK00007B/889

9 781801 212113